D0617544

The Ultimate Guide on
HOW TO SUCCEED IN
HIGH SCHOOL

30 fast tips every high school student and *parent* should know!

Robert R. Shallenberger

Why you should read this book

"Rob Shallenberger has hit a homerun with *How to Succeed in High School*! I have three teenagers and wow, is this information going to come in handy. I have already started discussing Rob's ideas with my teenagers to improve their High School experience. The neat thing about this book is that practically all of the recommendations apply to adults in whatever phase of life they're in! I plan to make this book part of all my children's reading. I highly recommend you do the same."

Dean Lee, Colonel USAF, High School Parent

"Rob has masterfully applied the analytical skills he honed as a fighter pilot to the high school battlefield! He has a knack for zeroing in on the key points in a complex problem, and he hit the bulls eye again here. The concepts in this book aren't just for high school either. Anybody who wants to supercharge their potential should read it today."

Shawn and Ulrika Cotton, Lt Colonel, USAF, and High School Parents

"*How to Succeed in High School* is an easy read. This book really helped improve my high school, work, church and sport life. I'm grateful I read this book while I still have some time left in high school. Every high school student needs to read this!"

Jenni Horner, Wasatch High School Student

"Timeless principles! If teens and parents work together to apply these simple tips, the future looks bright. The youth will become more than they ever thought possible!"

Vaughn and Tami Pyper, High School Parents

"High School can be hard. As a high school educator for the last six years I should know. *How to Succeed in High School* is the most complete guide for students and parents to find and experience success. I am recommending this book to all present and future high school students and their parents. Don't attempt to navigate high school without reading this book."

Brad Mathews, Morgan High School Teacher, Basketball and Football Coach, Parent

"*How To Succeed In High School* is an invaluable tool for students and families. Whether you're the student or a family member of a high school student, these tips provide relevant insights and patterns for success in making the journey of high school the 'best years' of life. The application of tips found within this book will not only lead students to achievement in their youth, but will also transfer high school experiences into a lifetime of success."

Jennifer Tanner, Dysart Unified School District Governing Board Member (Arizona), High School Parent

"*How to Succeed in High School* contains the essential ingredients for high school students to plan and execute methodologies to move to success at the next levels of their lives. It is easy to read and understand. I urge all high school students and their parents to read, discuss, plan, and act together implementing these powerful principles. You will be amazed at the results."

Superintendent Terry E. Shoemaker, Wasatch County School District, Utah

"I loved the book! It's short, to the point, and it gets a ton of useful information across to the reader. I also liked the fact that just by working on one of those tips, means you're working on another without knowing it. This book is great...I wish I would have had this when I was a freshman!"

Justin Gudmundson, Bonneville High School Student

Published by
Star Leadership LLC

Please visit www.BecomingYourBest.com

Manufactured in the United States of America, or in the United Kingdom when distributed elsewhere.

Shallenberger, Robert
The Ultimate Guide on How to Succeed in High School:
30 fast tips every high school student and parent should know!
ISBN Paperback: 978-0-9888459-0-9

Cover design and layout by Ali Majoka
http://www.facebook.com/grafikali.seven

For my amazing family:

Tonya, Robbie, Bella, Lana, and Clara

For my Parents:

Who helped instill in me a desire to continually work
on becoming a better person.

Thanks to friends who have inspired me,

both when I was young and the many years since.

Thanks to Brad for your help and assistance!

Congratulations on being an action taker! I'm glad you invested in this book. If you're currently in high school, planning to enter high school, or a parent who wants advice - this book is for you!

High school is a turning point in your life. This is a powerful, easy-to-read book designed to provide ideas and suggestions for high school students or their parents. *This isn't an in-depth, lengthy book. Rather, it's designed to provide fast and actionable tips on how to succeed.*

I've interviewed a large number of high school students in various grades. The advice and suggestions come from students who are "in the trenches" and who have seen the highs and lows high school offers. The advice comes from the students who are living it now and face the challenges of high school every day. This book is filled with 30 of the most influential and common suggestions given by those students.

Each tip or suggestion is important and this book is filled with some amazing advice. When I received feedback from the students, I was surprised at some of their answers and ideas - you may be as well.

I would suggest you start using these ideas as soon as you can. The sooner you make important decisions in your life the more successful you can be.

This is the book I wish someone would have given me when I was in high school!

Parents, these are great ideas to help guide your son or daughter in the right direction. It may even give you the answer you've been looking for to help your son or daughter. Parents and Administrators, if you'd like additional information on speaking engagements or private coaching, you can reference the *additional resources* in the back of the book.

To you, the student, good luck in high school! Enjoy the time and make the most of it.

Here's to your success...

Contents

Tip #1

Get a planner!

Quote: *"Good fortune is what happens when opportunity meets with planning."*

- Thomas Edison -

This was the #1 response when asked *"what do you wish someone would have told you when entering high school?"*

Learn how to organize and plan your week. High school has a busier schedule than middle school or junior high. You'll have a lot of extracurricular opportunities, homework, family activities, and other demands on your time. If you acquire a simple planner, you can take control of your schedule and you'll avoid those experiences where something slips through the cracks.

When you're organized, you're usually less stressed and you can stay on top of everything. If you're not sure how to plan and organize, then make the determination to learn.

You can go to *www.BecomingYourBest.com* for a simple tutorial on how to weekly plan and how to set goals. You can also download a free and powerful app called *Life Organizer* that will help you organize every area of your life - it will help with goal setting, weekly planning, to-do lists, and so on.

Tip #2

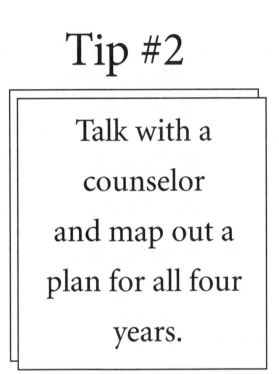

Talk with a
counselor
and map out a
plan for all four
years.

Quote: "Planning is bringing the future into the present so that you can do something about it now."

- Alan Lakein -

Find your school counselor. Sit down with the counselor and discuss all of the available classes at your school, then map out a general plan for all four years. If you have a specific university you would like to attend after high school, a counselor can tell you which classes will help you get into that university. A school counselor can be an invaluable resource!

Determine which classes are required and when you'll take them. You can then decide which electives might be most enjoyable and help you with your future. Some students have found themselves in summer school because they didn't take the classes they should have at the right time. You can avoid that with a solid plan.

Many students wish they took the time to create an outline of their classes before they were a junior or senior. When you choose your classes in the beginning, it will allow you to maximize your learning and take the classes you enjoy rather than being stuck in something that doesn't interest you. If you develop a plan, you'll reduce the stress in your life and you'll free up your energy to focus on other activities or ideas.

Tip #3

Develop a study plan.

Quote: *"Planning without action is futile; action without planning is fatal."*

\- Cornelius Fitchner -

Come up with a study plan to determine *when you'll study and do your homework and how much time you'll spend on it*. If you're just "shooting from the hip", high school might be a tough transition. You can be flexible and adjust your plan, but at least you'll have a plan!

Consider organizing a study group as part of your study plan. It's difficult to go from point A to point B without a plan. If you look online or in a bookstore, there are many good suggestions on how to develop a study plan. Try searching online for "*how to develop a homework study plan*." If you don't look online, a good start is to simply review the things you need to accomplish during the week, specifically your homework, and determine a block of time each day to do it. Once you've chosen a time, stick to your plan and get it done.

It will be easier to develop a study plan, if you do what was suggested previously and get an organizer or planner.

Tip #4

Learn
to
prioritize.

Quote: "The key is not to prioritize what's on your schedule, but to schedule your priorities."

- Stephen R. Covey -

This is closely tied to having a planner or organizer. This was one of the most common suggestions from the students I interviewed. You may have multiple things demanding your attention and you can only get so much done in that allotment of time. This is when you need to prioritize your tasks by what's most important down to what's least important.

Make a list of what you need to accomplish, with the most important at the top. Then, move down the list until you've accomplished everything you can in the allotted time. You can do this weekly or daily. Sometimes you may have to sacrifice the lower priority items to get the highest priority things done, that's alright.

By making a prioritized list, it allows you to get the highest priority items done, rather than fousing on the less important items and running out of time.

Tip #5

Don't procrastinate.

Quote: "Procrastination makes easy things hard, and hard things harder."

- Mason Cooley -

This is a habit you can develop now. Many adults are guilty of this and it's one of the greatest roadblocks to individual success.

You should never allow yourself to say the words, "I'll do this later" or "I'll do it in a little while". Be a doer and an action taker. Refer to your planner often and do it!

Some of the side effects of procrastination are: increased stress, incomplete homework, declining grades, and so on.

If you can master this simple, yet important habit, and eliminate procrastination, your odds of being successful throughout life will go up dramatically. It's not cool to procrastinate. You'll be much happier if you avoid procrastination.

Tip #6

Do your
homework early
and turn it in
on time.

*Quote: "Remember, action today can prevent a crisis
tomorrow."*

- Steve Shallenberger -

Start your homework as soon as you get it, rather than waiting until the due date. If you start early, you'll probably do a lot better.

If you get your homework done early and on time, your life will be less stressful and you'll actually have more free time.

When you get it done early, rather than waiting until the due date, it gives you a chance to review it without being rushed. When you review your homework and you're not rushed, you can catch the little things you may not have noticed the first time you did it.

Homework done early = less stress and better grades!

Tip #7

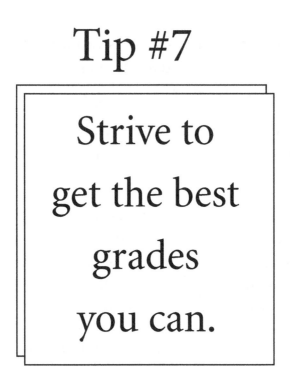

Strive to get the best grades you can.

Quote: "I do the very best I know how, the very best I can, and I mean to keep on doing so until the end."

- Abraham Lincoln -

When you set a goal for your GPA, write it down and keep it in a place where you can see it often.

You are important and you are capable of so much more than you might think. Set a specific goal for the GPA you would like to achieve, really stretch yourself.

I've met very few people who aren't capable of an "A", especially if they're willing to work with the teacher and put in the effort. Your GPA will make a huge difference in your future opportunities.

Unfortunately universities don't know you personally and, therefore, your GPA is one of the most important things universities look at to determine whether or not to accept you. As early as your freshman year, you will start opening and closing doors to your future. You may have a great personality, but if your GPA isn't high enough, many universities may not even consider you. Develop the habit now of opening doors for yourself by the actions you take today.

Tip #8

Write your goals and put them in a visible place.

Quote: *"Unless you have definite, precise, clearly set goals, you are not going to realize the maximum potential that lies within you."*

- Zig Ziglar -

This is very important! Put some thought into this.

Write your goals and keep them in a place where you can constantly see them. This simple act can improve your life in every way.

Choose some important goals related to each area of your life (as a son or daughter, friend, student, citizen or church member, etc.). List your goals for each area. As you write your goals, be specific. A good goal is something that's measurable and achievable, you can either say "yes" I did it or "no" I didn't.

You can certainly measure goals such as: I will join two separate clubs or organizations during my freshman year; I will read at least one inspiring book a month; I will work out at least three times a week for at least one hour per session; I will finish each year with at least a 3.8 GPA. These are examples of measurable and achievable goals.

Written goals give you a purpose and can inspire you to achieve great things!

Tip #9

Participate
in student
government, join
a club, or try out
for a sport.

*Quote: "Association with other human beings lures one
into self-observation."*

- Franz Kafka -

This is where many of your fun memories can be made and you'll develop many of the skills and talents you'll use later in life.

These associations may be just as valuable as any class you take. It keeps you involved and helps you grow. Find something you enjoy or something that might stretch you and help you develop your talents.

The more involved you are, the more fun you'll probably have in school. Bigger high schools have almost every type of club or sports you can imagine. If you're at a smaller high school and it doesn't have a club or sports team, consider creating a club or group that has to do with your interests.

Tip #10

Have
fun.

Quote: "People rarely succeed unless they have fun at what they are doing."

- Dale Carnegie -

High school can be fun if you let it be.

Get involved, don't worry too much about the drama, and enjoy the moment. It's important to laugh and remember that there's a time to be serious and a time to play. High school provides plenty of time to enjoy yourself, whether at a school play, sporting event, or other extracurricular activity.

Always remember, you can have clean fun without doing something illegal or participating in activities that might cause hurt to someone else.

Choose your friends carefully and you'll make some wonderful memories.

Tip #11

Learn from your homework.

Quote: "We ought to be ten times as hungry for knowledge as for food for the body."

- Henry Beecher -

You'll be doing homework from 9th grade through 12th grade. You can either go through the motions and put in the minimum required effort for the grade, or you can actually learn from what you're studying.

If you make an effort to really learn the information, high school will be far more enjoyable than if you go through the motions. If you actually try to learn from your homework, you'll find it much more enjoyable than if you do it, just to do it.

There's not really any specific steps to take, rather it's a mindset you can develop now that will pay huge dividends throughout your life. If you're doing homework anyway, get as much out of it as you can!

Tip #12

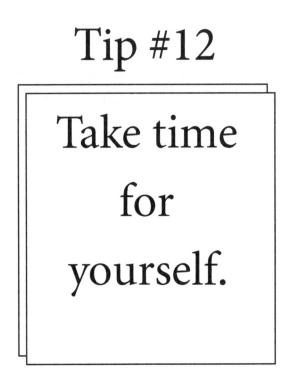

Take time
for
yourself.

Quote: "The more a person meditates upon good thoughts, the better will be their world and the world at large."

- Confucius -

Try and take at least a few minutes each day to simply be alone and meditate.

You're going to be busy with your high school schedule. You should take some time to contemplate and reflect on your life. Technology, friends, homework, sports, and other activities will demand your time...you need to take some time for yourself!

Sometimes it's the quiet moments where the greatest learning takes place. There's a lot you can learn when you take a few minutes to pray, meditate, or ponder. It allows you to refocus and opens the windows of inspiration. It was interesting to hear from students that this really helped them relax and be more successful.

This life is fast paced, we all need to take a few minutes to slow down and pray, meditate, or ponder for a few minutes. Determine when you can do this during the week, otherwise it may slip away from you.

Tip #13

Take a lot of pictures.

Quote: "Of all of our inventions for mass communication, pictures still speak the most universally understood language."

- Author Unknown -

Not only will this help you remember your experiences, but when you apply for a scholarship, pictures help! If you have pictures of you serving in the community or helping others, those can help you down the road.

There are a lot of opportunities to use pictures later in life, outside of educational institutions. Pictures will also help you remember some of the fun experiences you had during high school.

If you take pictures, find a way to back them up on your computer so they don't get lost. People have lost hundreds and even thousands of pictures, simply because the files weren't backed up on another drive or disk.

Tip #14

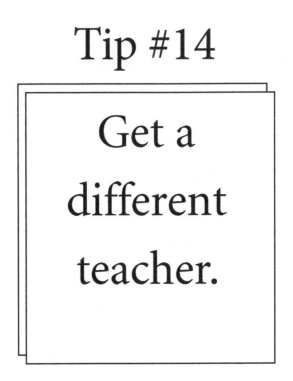

Get a different teacher.

Quote: "A teacher affects eternity; he or she can never tell where their influence stops."

- Henry Adams -

This should be the last resort. If you don't get along well with a particular teacher, consider talking with someone in the administration office and possibly move to a different class. This is important if you feel like you are not learning from your teacher. Typically, grades and attitude improve when there's a positive relationship with the teacher.

Sometimes it's true, we simply have better chemistry with certain people. A great teacher has the ability to connect and inspire.

Do your best to work with your original assigned teacher and try to sort through the challenges before you request to switch teachers. However, once you've done your best and it still isn't working, you may be better served by requesting a change. As a reminder, if you request to switch teachers, this should be one of your last resorts.

Tip #15

People might

be mean and

take advantage

of you

- don't worry!

Quote: "It's not the situation. It's your reaction to the situation."

- Robert Conklin -

This isn't something to be scared of or something you should worry about. Both at this age and later in life, it can be a tough world. Sometimes we wish people would treat each other with more kindness. Instead of being nervous about the way you might be treated by others, determine who you will be and how you'll respond. You can determine how you will treat others.

If something isn't right or if there is some kind of bullying, you should IMMEDIATELY talk with your teacher or someone in the administrative office. When you tell a teacher or administrator, you're helping yourself, others, and the person who's being the bully. You shouldn't let people take advantage of you.

Determine now your response to the actions of others and you'll empower yourself, rather than allowing others to control you. Something that might help you is to write your desired response in a journal or role play with someone you trust, such as a parent.

Determine now to take the high road, no matter how others may treat you.

Tip #16

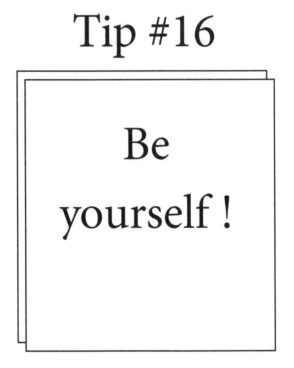

Be
yourself !

Quote: "To be yourself in a world that is constantly trying to make you something else is the greatest accomplishment."

- Ralph Waldo Emerson -

You'll find all kinds of outside influences and "friends" trying to convince you what and who you're supposed to be. You are unique. You have wonderful talents. There isn't another "*you*" in this world.

Dare to stand alone and be unique. Learn from the good and make it better. Learn from the good of others and incorporate that into your life. Don't compare yourself to others. Never try to be someone you're not.

Determine now that you'll never do anything as a result of "peer pressure". You can make a difference in the world, focus on the positive and shun the negative.

Tip #17

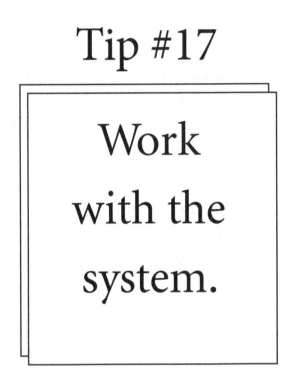

Work with the system.

Quote: *"Do what you can, with what you have, where you are."*

- Theodore Roosevelt -

Most would agree that our school systems are far from perfect. However, it's what we have and there are still wonderful opportunities in most schools.

You'll have to take some classes which might feel as if they have little real-life application. There will also be some classes which feel like they really prepare you well for life. If you're taking a required class and you feel like there isn't much real-life application, choose to do your best and search for a way to let it help you grow. You'll get out of something what you put into it.

When you're choosing your elective classes, really put forward some effort and choose classes you think will be useful to you in the professional world. The more skills and knowledge you acquire now, the better off you'll be later. When you're trying to determine your schedule and you're stuck trying to decide between two classes, consider choosing the one that will give you the most real-life application.

Tip #18

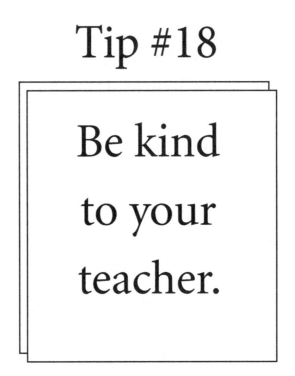

Be kind to your teacher.

Quote: *"Three things in human life are important. The first is to be kind. The second is to be kind. And the third is to be kind."*

-Henry James -

You certainly want the teacher on your side. Oftentimes, a person receives from others what they send out in their words and actions. There's a saying which says, "*you reap what you sow*".

It's always easier to be kind and help someone when they are kind to you. It's more challenging to be kind to someone who doesn't appear to be kind to you. Either way, consider leaving a nice note for your teacher, buy him or her an apple, or leave a small gift to say "*thank you*".

It doesn't have to be complex, just be nice and periodically do something kind for your teachers - it will pay off in the long-run. Small acts of kindness can go a long way!

Tip #19

Don't sweat the small stuff.

Quote: "Don't sweat the small stuff...and it's all small stuff."

- Richard Carlson -

Tip #21

Treat others the way you want to be treated.

Quote: "I've learned that people will forget what you said, people will forget what you did, but people will never forget how you made them feel."

- Mary Angelou -

Sometimes we worry about the small things and forget there are more important things to spend our time and energy thinking about.

Don't worry about how someone looked at you or whether a certain person wants to hang out, just focus on the big picture. What seems like a big deal now is something you probably won't remember in a few years. Remember your goals and keep your focus on them.

In 10 years from now you'll forget most of those small things, don't sweat the small stuff. If it's something that bothers you, learn to let it go and turn your energy to the important things in your life.

One way to let it go is to use your computer or piece of paper and write down the 10 most important things in your life. Think of specific things you can do to improve those areas and as soon your mind turns to focus on those areas of improvement, the smaller things seem to lose their significance.

Tip #20

Enjoy dating.

Quote: "My boyfriend used to ask his mother, How can I find the right woman for me? She would answer, Don't worry about finding the right woman - concentrate on becoming the right man."

- Author Unknown -

42

This is a fun time of life and you should enjoy dating when you're ready to date and you have your parents' permission.

One of the most enjoyable things you can do is go on group dates. Use caution in exclusive dating at this age, there's rarely a reason to get serious with someone while in high school.

There are so many good people to meet and have fun with. This is the time to date many different people and identify what traits you would like in a husband or wife someday.

If you have an exclusive boyfriend or girlfriend, you run the risk of missing out on many memorable activities with others. In addition, be very careful about the moral choices you make while dating, they will affect the rest of your life!

43

Life will smile on those who are kind to others!

Open the door for others, give people complements, help someone in need, pick up someone's papers or books when they fall on the floor. Always look around for opportunities to help others.

A lot of people act like everything is fine, when in reality they might be hurting inside. You can be the person to help make the difference, with a small act of kindness. Do you remember when someone did something nice for you? How did it make you feel?

It only takes one person to make a difference! You can be the difference.

Tip #22

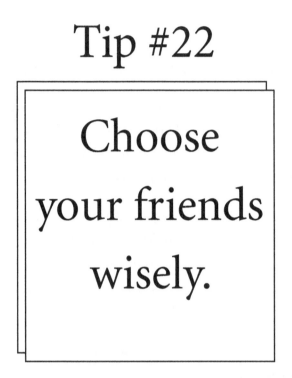

Choose your friends wisely.

Quote: "Be careful the environment you choose for it will shape you; be careful the friends you choose for you will become like them."

- W. Clement Stone -

If you look around, the saying *"birds of a feather flock together"* is usually true. Choose friends who inspire you and make you want to improve and be a better person. We generally tend to become like those who we associate with.

If your "friends" invite you to do things you know aren't right, you should look for other friends. If they invite you to skip class, experiment with drugs or pornography, swear, or other degrading things - find new friends. You can still be kind to everyone, but choose carefully those people who you spend your time with.

Ask yourself :

1. Do my friends inspire me to be a better person?

2. Do my friends help me feel like I can achieve great things?

3. Do my friends help me feel like I should raise my goals and dreams?

If you answered *yes*, then these are the types of friends you should find, friends who instill these feelings inside of you! You can and should also be that kind of friend to others.

The same principle applies to adults later in life, you can develop the habit now to associate with people who inspire you.

Tip #23

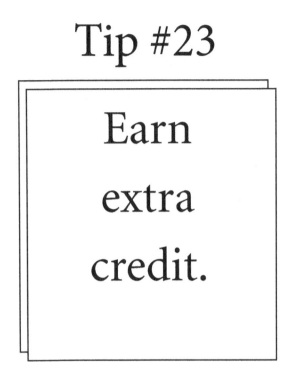

Earn

extra

credit.

Quote: "*No one ever attains very eminent success by simply doing what is required of him; it is the amount and excellence of what is over and above the required, that determines the greatness of ultimate distinction.*"

- Charles Francis Adams -

Anytime you have the opportunity to earn extra credit in a class, take it (as long it doesn't take away from something that's a higher priority).

There are a lot of reasons to do extra credit: it helps your overall grade, the teacher notices the effort you put into it, and you will learn something in the process. It could be at the end of the semester or term, when that little piece of extra credit was the percentage that made the difference.

You can develop the mindset of an achiever right now. It's about going the extra mile, taking an extra step when it isn't required. It's that final push, doing just a little bit more. This is just as much about your attitude towards life, as it is about any other benefit.

Tip #24

Get your
sleep... go to
bed early and
rise early.

*Quote: "Without enough sleep, we all become tall
two-year olds."*

- JoJo Jensen -

There are studies which show if you go to bed early and get up early, you'll generally do better on tests and perform better in other activities.

On a school night, try and get at least a solid eight hours of sleep and you should notice that you're more alert, happy, and ready to take on the challenges of the day. You generally don't help yourself if you only get 4 - 5 hours of sleep.

It's easy to get into a routine of little sleep. In most cases, you'll do better and feel better when you get a good rest.

Tip #25

Be kind to your family members.

Quote: *"Our most basic instinct is not for survival, but for family. Most of us would give our own life for the survival of a family member, yet we lead our daily life too often as if we take our family for granted."*

- Paul Pearshall -

Behind almost every successful high school student is a caring father or mother (or both).

Whether you think your parents are cool or not, remember they invest a lot of time and money into you. They want you to be successful. They care about you. They love you.

Some high school students feel like it's not cool to express your love to your parents. Please thank them and tell them you love them...you'll never be sorry. Remember, you only have a limited amount of time with family members, so make the best of the time you have.

If you express your love for them and say thank you often, then you should be congratulated. If not, please find a way (today) to say the words "I love you" to your parents. You will never regret this simple piece of advice!

Tip #26

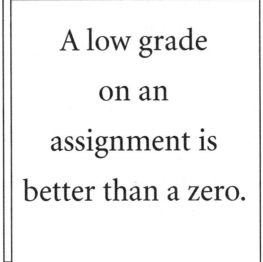

A low grade

on an

assignment is

better than a zero.

Quote: "Instead of doing nothing because I'm overwhelmed, today I will do something, even if it's small, because it will be one step closer to my goal."

- Author Unknown -

This is a very important lesson: *It's better to turn in something than nothing.*

At some point in your high school career, you may realize you have a homework assignment that's due and somehow you forgot about it or it slipped through the cracks.

A quality assignment is best, but if for some reason you don't have time and the assignment is due, it's better to put together something and get some points, than to turn in nothing and get a zero. If you get some points, at least there's been something contributed to a better grade. The best way to get a zero on an assignment is to turn in nothing.

Remember, some points are better than no points.

Tip #27

Forgive yourself.
Learn from
the past, but
look to the future.

Quote: "Life can only be understood backwards, but it must be lived forwards."

- Soren Kierkegaard -

Despite what anyone may think or tell you, the future can be bright and glorious! You will determine what happens today and tomorrow. Let the past be the past, learn from it, but leave it in the past.

We all make mistakes and do things we wish we wouldn't have done. That's part of being human. It's important to forgive others, but also to forgive yourself.

Learn from your mistakes, but don't dwell on them and let them drag you down. Once you've learned those lessons, turn your focus to the present and the future. You can make an enormous difference in the lives of others, and it's easier to do this if you're not depressed or bogged down because of the past.

Tip #28

If you have
a challenge and
you feel lost,
ask for help.

Quote: "The strong individual is the one who asks for help when they need it."

- Rona Barrett -

It's OK to ask for help!

High school has all kinds of challenges. If you're ever feeling down, especially if you feel like you can't go on, talk with someone. There's never a reason to give up on yourself, and there's always reasons to keep going.

Nearly every school has a counselor and they would love to talk with you. If you don't feel comfortable talking with a counselor, find someone you trust and talk with them. If you feel comfortable talking with your parents, they can listen to your concerns and, in most cases, be willing to help.

Remember, never give up. When you feel down, whatever is causing those feelings will pass and the sun will rise again. There is ALWAYS hope!

Tip #29

Figure out what options are out there for you and apply for scholarships.

Quote: *"A wise man will make more opportunities than he finds."*

- Francis Bacon -

Go out and make the effort to search for scholarships you may qualify to receive. One of your primary objectives in high school is to learn to open as many doors as possible.

You can use the internet to search for scholarships and apply as early as you can. Sometimes, the application process should start as early as your junior year. Every year, there are a few scholarships which go unused because nobody applied for them. I personally know of one large scholarship that was unused last year because nobody applied for it.

Even if you think you don't qualify for a scholarship, search the internet and you'll be amazed at the different types of scholarships offered. There are scholarships with certain restrictions such as race, religion, ethnicity, etc. You might qualify for a lot more than you think you do! There are a lot of scholarships awarded by private organizations and donors that have nothing to do with the university you choose.

Make the effort to search and apply and the financial reward may well be worth your work!

Tip #30

Apply to
universities early
and call to verify
they have a complete
application.

Quote: *"Do today what others won't, so tomorrow, you
can do what others can't."*

- Brian Rogers Loop -

It would be a tragedy if you thought you had all the necessary paperwork submitted to the university of your choice, then you were declined entry because there was something missing in your application.

Submit an application early to as many universities as reasonably possible (you can always decline later). Once you've submitted the application, follow up with the university and get a confirmation that all your paperwork has been correctly submitted and received.

The earlier you start the submission process, the better. It's one of the best ways to avoid a "submission crisis".

Once you've submitted your application and verified its receipt, you can sit back and wait for the big day!

Conclusion:

I hope these fast and powerful tips have been helpful. If you implement these simple ideas, your ability to succeed in high school can skyrocket.

I suggest you don't just read this book once and then stash it away in the closet. If you read it several times, you'll pick up on ideas you may have missed the first time.

It's a fast, easy read and may spur an idea in the moment you need it. You never know when one of these simple ideas becomes the catalyst for change or improvement in your life.

If you would like more ideas and something to really take it to the next level, I enroll a limited number of youth to personally coach and mentor. This has proven to be very successful. You can find out more information about the personal coaching program in the additional resources at the end of the book.

Good luck in this fun and exciting phase of life!

Your Friend,

Rob Shallenberger

Additional Resources

For Parents:

Have you ever struggled to get your son or daughter motivated?

Have you ever felt like it would be helpful to have someone who could assist you to inspire and motivate your teenager?

Many business executives around the world use a personal coach for numerous reasons, a few of which are to lift, motivate, teach, and hold accountable. How valuable would this be for your son or daughter?

Rob loves to work with and motivate youth and help them move towards accomplishing their dreams. He's developed a <u>powerful coaching program</u> that can motivate and instill a sense of drive and commitment in your child. If you'd like to learn more about Rob's life-changing coaching program, for your child, please contact him using the information below.

For School Administrators:

Rob has taught and coached youth, as well as Fortune 500 executives, around the world. He can bring to bear an exciting background as a fighter pilot and entrepreneur to motivate and inspire your students. Contact Rob if you'd like a personal and unforgettable experience for your students. To contact Rob for a speaking engagement, please contact him using the information below.

Rob Shallenberger
3450 South 2900 West
Heber City, UT 84032
Rob@BecomingYourBest.com
801-367-3759

CPSIA information can be obtained at www.ICGtesting.com
Printed in the USA
BVOW08s0840090714

358544BV00013B/199/P

9 780988 845909